Dedication

This book is dedicated to those who read it, in the hope that man recognizes his rights and stands up for them.

Acknowledgements

I want to thank

My sister,
Dr. Diana Pengitore, ND, freelance translator, and American Translator Association (ATA) member, for her expert translation from German to English, which was long overdue.

My brother-in-law,
Dr. Frank Pengitore, Ed. D., for his editorial expertise in bringing this publication forth.

Another excellent publication is *My Philosophy*. *My Philosophy* is the first book **in a five-part series** from the book *Philosophy of Life - The Book of Basics*. This complete series is available in German. The remaining four books (*Learning how to Learn, Learning How to Understand; A Happy Relationship; To Endure Life - The Bible of the 21st Century;* and, *Past Life Regression - Introduction and Brief Guide*) will be published in English in the future.

Wolfgang Fries

Human Rights and Obligations - Revised

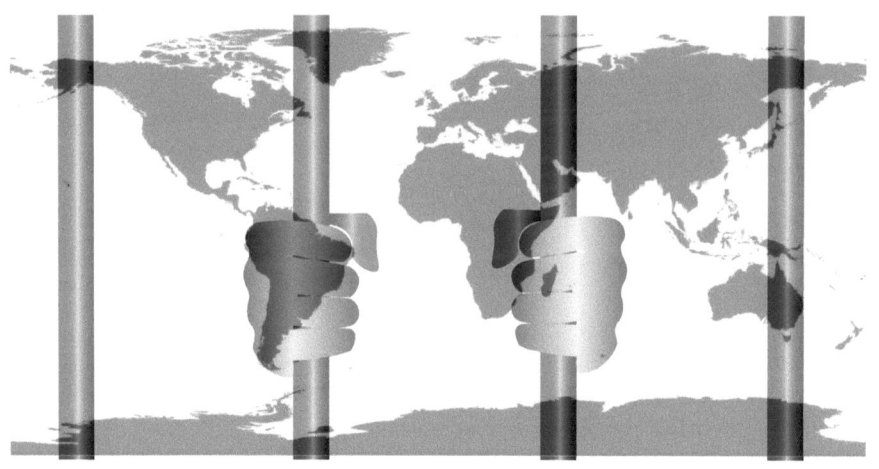

Imprint

Book design and typeset:
Wolfgang Fries
Contact: Friesway@online.de

Translator: Dr. Diana M. Pengitore, ND
Editor: Dr. Frank Pengitore, Ed. D.

Production and publishing:
BoD - Books on Demand
In de Tarpen 42
22848 Norderstedt; Deutschland

ISBN: 978-3-7481-3006-2
Handbook, softcover
1. Edition

© 2018 for the content Wolfgang Fries
© 2018 Books on Demand GmbH, Norderstedt

Bibliografische Information der Deutschen Nationalbibliothek
Die Deutsche Nationalbibliothek verzeichnet diese Publikation in der Deutschen Nationalbibliografie; detaillierte bibliografische Daten sind im Internet über http://dnb.d-nb.de abrufbar.
(The book is listed in the German Nationalbibliografie; detailed information is available at: http://dnb.d-nb.de)

Important note to the reader:

Take great care in reading this text in order not to skip words that you do not understand. If you do not understand a sentence or text, there is a word or there are words that you did not understand, or you have a false definition for a word.

In this text, words marked with an asterisk (*) are explained in the glossary on page 27; however, they are just the definitions of the words as they are used in the corresponding sentence. Words often have many definitions and to reach a complete understanding of a word, it is recommended that you consult a good dictionary.

Table of Contents

Foreword

The word law finds its roots in the Indo-Germanic, reg-, meaning "to erect, to straighten." Therefore, the law should serve to help human beings in taking the right action. It should lead human beings to getting along with one another and should regulate the authorities from state to citizen and from citizen to state, or even from state to state. Human rights are intended that people can live!

In 1948, the General Assembly of the United Nations issued the "General Assembly of Declaration of Human Rights." Well, I did not entirely agree with that decree and as we have a right to freedom of speech, I wrote my views about it down.

Any information one receives and puts into his construct of thought leads to the expansion of one's point of view. Even if the information is not quite as good, or exact, or even wrong, one can still strengthen his own point of view by recognizing the wrong information and by improving things. Through a lively exchange of ideas, one can contribute in finding better principles that lead to a better existence.

Any system of state, law, or religion that disregards reason and the freedom of choice of the people and tries to enforce rules and laws under coercion, violence or manipulation, without appealing to reason and people's ability to learn, shall be damned! Life itself has its laws, and if people violate these laws, then they are punishing themselves. Forcing human beings to do anything that violates the laws of life degrades their reason and encourages people to do things secretly, even to evade responsibility, thus escaping punishment from the law. It does not lead individuals to admit to their act and to work on themselves, resulting in a different mindset.

If the human being knows the laws of existence, then he would stand up for the laws and make sure that others would stand up for them as well. Not to act will result in laws and penalties in a world where people will have a hard time being happy. No law of the world has ever made Man to be a better Man, but his ability to learn and his reason made it! Any system of education that does not promote reason and a human being's ability to learn and does not teach the laws of life shall be damned! For human beings' reason and their ability to learn, as well as the laws of life, are the only guarantor that people can live with human dignity!

Human Rights and Obligations - Revised*

Now, of what consciousness, of what level of knowledge, of what zeitgeist* does one write? When one writes about something, one should know about it, one should have experience and have experienced for themselves how things are. It is of no use if one throws old theories that have never worked into a pot with newer, different theories that have not yet worked, cooking them and thinking afterwards, that one has created a healing miracle.

If one writes something about human rights, one should know something about humanity. Furthermore, one should represent the framework conditions in which human rights are implemented. Rights change when the framework conditions change. In a barbaric environment* the rights and obligations are formulated differently compared to a civilization that is dominated by machines, computers, science and money.

The barbarian will not respect any rights and obligations; he will simply take what he needs to live or desires and not pursue any of his obligations. He is only able to do this because he is stronger than anyone else. In comparison to the animal kingdom, there is not much difference. Barbarism will always be the cause of war; there will never be peace and quiet. Thus, one's own life is endangered every day.

Do not believe that today's "civilization" is far from barbarism. To be forced to do something through brute violence or through financial hardship/inferiority makes no difference. In the final analysis, the individual must bow to the greater power! Therefore, the state with its laws and the police have power over people and can force them into a certain behavior or punish and imprison them when they do not obey. The question regarding the laws is whether they are right or wrong concerning the existence of the individual and the state's ability to operate, or whether it is only an attempt to suppress the individual within the state.

Socialism and communism were rejected because they denied the individual the right to have property, putting the welfare of the group above the welfare of the individual. Furthermore, it was ignored that the welfare of the individual eventually signified the welfare of the group or the state. Today, in our democracy we are on that exact path. Most people have little money to afford property and are forced through financial pressure to constantly perform a task that in the end benefits the state through taxation, the means by which the needs of the group are addressed.

A government should govern people, exactly what the word "govern" means. Ruling does not mean to pass a multitude of laws that no one knows anymore, leaving one to sit down and wait for the outcome of the country's general development. The welfare of a country and its population requires action that ensures the existence and happiness for every individual within society, so that from the individual parts a well-functioning total enterprise arises.

The Right to Physical Integrity and Physical Welfare

The governments of the world and their citizens should be able to ensure physical integrity and physical well-being in the 21st century.

Everyone in this civilization should be granted all the basic needs for existence and have enough protection for weather conditions, food*, and an average standard of living, as is the case for the most of Central Europe.

Medical care, which includes medicines and aid as part of the basic needs, should be available to everyone regardless of monetary means - medicine should not be a profit-oriented branch of industry for which a small fortune is required.

The Right to Mental Integrity and Mental Welfare

This addresses the thoughts and the emotional state of the human being. An environment that conveys fears of existence or threatens any loss to people, be it through an insecure job or a haphazard political leadership, leads to the decline of the person's emotional level.

Stress, meaning mental pressure, often is the cause of illness, as specified many times over by medicine. It is the mental pressure that causes the person to worry about, or even to lose, something. In the business world, time or money is often restricted and; therefore, it is not possible to do good work. As a result, the occupational burden is carried over to the family life, causing much tension, again resulting in worry and in not be able to satisfy the needs of the family. The result being the dissolution of the family.

A safe and insightful environment gives human beings a feeling of safety, which reduces mental pressure. In fact, human beings themselves do not have enough knowledge and resources to face mental pressure. It requires a specific environment, guidelines and practices to ensure people's mental integrity and mental wellness because thoughts lead to action and a hectic and an unjust world by no means leads to a relaxed and prudent lifestyle!

The Right to Education

Education outlines the mental framework necessary for an individual to lead a life. Hence, education does just that: It provides the individual with a mental foundation and the principles to lead a happy life within the framework described in this book. Education should ensure that people can analyze the problems of existence well and eventually can make a rational decision – something modern school education is incapable of doing for whatever reason. Education should lead to an understanding, so that the person understands what he does and why he does it.

Education should be a pleasurable experience for people because they will have greater knowledge, a better understanding and; therefore, be able to help themselves better. Regarding educational institutions, it is not beneficial to cram people full of stuff that they cannot use, putting them on the verge of a nervous breakdown shortly before their final exam, only because they think that they cannot recollect the material as required, which can lead to *fears of existence** if they fail the exam!

The Right to Truth and Transparency

Everyone has the right to his own opinion, and everyone can express his own opinion but without annoying, vilifying, or hurting someone in a degrading way. Facts*are presented in an open, complete, truthful, understandable, and knowledgeable manner, without attracting attention in a provoking way to flare up tempers. Therefore, try and stay with the truth!

Information should be valuable and not serve to keep people ignorant and manipulated*, as is currently the case with the media. Announcing that somewhere in the world something bad has happened, only intimidates a person, making him insecure. Valuable information helps people to better deal with their everyday lives and to solve problems; it is not simply to entertain, to eliminate boredom, or to support an increase in advertising revenue.

Any information should be presented in an intelligible way, so that it can be understood with simple general education, as it is taught until the end of high school. Anyone who encrypts information by an intricate sentence structure or complex choice of words, or selectively reports only information that supports a particular cause or political agenda wants to either oppress the people or tell a lie. To deprive the person of freedom starts with a lack of understanding of himself or his surroundings. Only the person who understands, can be free.

The Right to a Civilized Life

Treat others the way you would like to be treated! When one annoys others by the way he treats them, he will reap discontent and create an environment in which no joy can develop. Try to give others the freedom that they need, so that they can be themselves because no one likes to be constantly patronized!

The Right to a Mentally Sane Government

A government is not a puppet show. The members of a government consist of intelligent and reasonable experts. No one can require a decision to solve a problem from a non-expert in which expertise is necessary. Likewise, no citizen can be asked to appoint qualified staff for a government. A person has to qualify for a job before being employed.

A sane government cares about managing a country; it takes care that enough projects exist to give work to its citizens. It takes care that the conditions in the country improve. A government issues laws to establish an existence in which there is a balanced relationship between freedoms and barriers that allows people to get along with each other without major injuries. It issues laws to make things possible and not to stop positive things because of even more restrictions and complexities!

As long as governments only talk and do nothing, don't put effective funding programs for the country into action, talk about wealth when large segments of the population are impoverished*, do not understand money and fight each other, one cannot talk about mentally sane governments!

A government does not haggle about money; a government governs the money and not the money the government. It takes action to solve upcoming problems quickly - it is not debated. A government should give its citizens a feeling of security that shows that it cares about their concerns and demonstrates functionality through its actions.

The existence of a government is justified only by the citizens, otherwise there is no reason for a government. A government has all of the power in the state and shall use it selflessly for the governing of the country and welfare of the people.

The Right to a Mentally Sane Humanity

Well, the mind of humankind is contaminated by religions, ideologies *, education, laws, prejudices and false ideas about right and wrong.

Mental health primarily has two factors*: (a) the fundamental comprehension about right and wrong and (b) the freedom of action. Freedom of action means that the human being does not act compulsively. Wars, religious madness or other crimes, furthermore obsessive jealousy, greed or other compulsions and fears are the exact basis for an inversion* of these two factors.

Every human being should feel obligated to gain a basic understanding about right and wrong and to take measures to increase his freedom of action, only then can there be a sane humanity. Mental health furthermore includes being fully aware of one's awareness so that one can act responsibly.

Misguided mental practices that do not lead the human being to a self-determined and self-responsible action are the way into the abyss and make the human being into a puppet of the treating "therapists" - be it psychology, psychiatry or the shaman with his dance, oracle*, crystal balls, astrology, tarot cards*, etc.

Psychotropic substances, meaning mind-altering substances, such as illegal drugs, alcohol, and medicines reduce accountability and, when ingested in large quantities, can pose a danger to the person or the environment. Psychotropic substances should only be used to avert major discomfort and only in a restricted environment. The human being can only act and react accordingly when he is in full possession of his mental powers.

Strong emotions thwart rational actions. Mentally sane also means being able to keep emotions at bay so as not to cause damage through emotional, hasty actions. The human being should learn to deal with his emotions.

Mental health means distinguishing between the past and the present and being able to free oneself from the past! Past experiences seem to keep the human being in the past and cloud his judgment: "What was bad yesterday is not good today either!" If someone made a mistake at some point that mistake will be held against him, even years later, condemning him. Often one does not get a second chance, even though one has learned from his mistake, regrets it and would certainly not do it again! However, there are also those with fixed behavior, who make the same mistake again and again - no freedom of action!

Common sense includes: careful observation, correct decision and appropriate action. Comments like, "It's none of my business," "I do not care," and "I cannot change it" demonstrate an attitude of ignorance and a lack of responsibility. It is unreasonable, insane and the way into the abyss!

The Right to an Affordable Life
There must be a balance between revenue and expenditure. If one cannot cover his expenses due to low income, then he cannot lead an independent life.

Due to price wars and rationalization*, the earning potential is becoming less and less. This requires legal regulation, which mandates maximum working hours and a sufficient minimum wage. Furthermore, costs for basic necessities of existence must be in proportion to a minimum wage income. Therefore, it cannot be that rents are increasing just to satisfy man's greed.

The Right to Have a Place to Live
People have a right to a home. They are here now and want to live. It should be noted that care must be taken when choosing the environment in which a person wishes to live. There is still racial unrest due to a lack of tolerance, so to prevent conflict, one should settle in a community where there is either high racial tolerance or only slight differences from person to person, be it in appearance or in mental orientation. Also, of importance, the possibility must exist for people to join a community, to have their own country with their own laws!

The Right to Work

Work is not just an activity undertaken to earn a living. Some may whine about how beautiful the world would be without work because they would rather go on vacation. But to have no work that gives the person a direction and an orderly daily routine, will make the person depressed*. There is probably nothing worse than to feel useless and to have no goal in mind. It is often the case that the retired person dies or lets himself go. Many long-term unemployed are frustrated and demoralized.

A task gives a person the momentum to complete the job and to achieve something in life. Therefore, work is a therapeutic measure to uphold the morale of people and, by extension, the nation. People who do something meaningful in life for the common good are highly satisfied. It is nice to have a feeling of helping someone and to realize, that through an activity, things improve and thereby enrich life.

A government should direct the power of people meaningfully by starting projects and by providing work to the citizens so that they can develop their own country and keep it in order.

The Right to Happiness

The person is happy when his will is not opposed by insurmountable barriers, so that if he wants to have something, he can get it, or if he wants to get rid of something, he can get rid of it. He also does not want that something is simply taken from or imposed upon him.

Received commitments must be fulfilled; one should keep his promises. As far as happiness is concerned, there are often two sides where the other side is not influenced or perhaps difficult to influence. Misfortune often has to do with the fact that the person is mentally unable to release something. The matter is a thought in his head and he is unable to let go of the thought or to exchange one thought with another. This would be the personal issue of the individual, which can be adequately encountered through mental processes.

However, there are extrinsic* factors, e.g. external factors that influence the happiness of the person. The state can, through legislation, assure that when complying with certain rules, one is entitled to an existence within a society.

The laws of the state are usually written to promote peace within the society, whereby the state contributes to the happiness of its citizens. Laws should be created by the state so that the citizen can implement his will within the state without the laws presenting an insurmountable barrier. One can make things simple or complicated!

To be happy mainly requires theoretical foundations which can be applied by the person and these foundations should be developed and known to everyone.

One must work on his own happiness! To be happy in life is the highest guarantee one can have to ensure that he feels joy in his existence. A person who is unhappy and does not feel joy in his existence is not only a risk to himself but also to society. Who would start and destroy things or handle them carelessly that are the source of his happiness?

The Right to a Have a Family

What would a child be without the protection of his parents? The family is the main societal unit of a nation, even of all mankind. For without the family, it is not possible to have a functioning society. Thus, every human being has a naturally given impulse for procreation; it is a large part in a human's emotional life. The human being's decisions originate mostly from his emotional life.

If a person is denied the gratification of his emotional life, he becomes dissatisfied and can turn to actions not based on reason. The family itself should be supported, so that life can live on from children to grandchildren. The government of a country should pay attention to the functioning ability of the family, so that a family can exist despite economic and temporal pressure.

The Right to a Group

The individual wants to be active and to have contact with his fellow human beings. A group is a community of interests that serves to entertain and helps people solve common problems. The professional life often is a group activity. People that belong in a group are significantly more effective than the individual. Without the collective effort of a group, a nation cannot be governed because a group strengthens and supports the individual.

What would a person be without a group in which he can have friendship? Many things cannot be done alone and, so it is valuable when someone lends a helping hand or when things are undertaken together as a community. How much more joy can the individual have when he is active in a likeminded community, rather than to be locked in within his own four walls?

The Right to Humanity

Human beings are encountered on all continents of the planet, with everyone being a part of this whole, a part of humanity. Human beings are dependent upon each other for things, like raw materials or products that are found only in a certain part of the world due to their resources, surroundings , or weather conditions. Humanity can grow by helping each other as a group and by getting along with one another.

Who does not enjoy travelling to another country to get to know something different and to form friendships? It is exciting and entertaining when people compete in a sporting event, be it in football or in the Olympic games, when almost everyone is watching on television or travelling to the actual event.

International relations should be strengthened, be it through student exchange programs or the projects of interrelated countries, so that the neighbor does not appear strange!

The Right to Have Animals and Plants

This does not mean that everyone should occupy themselves with livestock or the keeping of plants. It does mean, that at a bare minimum, care must be taken to preserve the animal kingdom and the plant world, as these also ensure the survival of humanity and their home on earth.

In a well populated world, it is easy to assign to some people during their working hours the task of taking care of the animal kingdom and the plant world. There will be enough people who will do this with joy and devotion because they are aware of its importance.

The Right to a Clean Environment

People who do not wash themselves, stink and are an Eldorado* for pathogens. It is, therefore, of utmost importance that people maintain good hygiene. Contamination is the source of illness and decline. During the Middle Ages in Europe, fleas carrying the Yersinia pestis bacteria infested rats who were responsible for spreading the pestilence* (bubonic plague), killing millions. However, people helped spread disease by throwing away food, thereby supplying the rats with enough provisions to live

Trash must be discarded properly and precious raw materials that can be recycled separated from it Also, before the production of any product, it is necessary to contemplate how the materials that are being utilized are to be re-used in the production process after the product is consumed! Trash that cannot be reutilized in some way or another should not be allowed to accumulate, even after burning, so that the ashes or exhausts will not cause damage or harm.

Trash is a big problem of the modern world. It is not that the resources for elimination do not exist, it is the fact that the person with his own action is contributing to the downfall of his own environment by not properly taking care of the environment and by adding to its pollution, resulting in his own destruction.

Regarding money, it is not acceptable to forego a reasonable cost for disposal of toxic waste and to allow poisonous exhausts to be emitted into the air. It is not acceptable that trash gets dumped into the ocean, where it enters the food chain, and pollutes nature to the point where it presents itself as a radioactive fish, eventually landing on one's own plate! ☹ The "Great Pacific garbage patch," is a huge collection of floating plastic trash halfway between Hawaii and California that extends over an area estimated to be the size of Texas. The patch contains mostly plastic fragments, often microscopic, that have been trapped by the currents of the North Pacific ("Great Pacific," n.d.). Only recently, have attempts been made to clean it up. It is not acceptable to have drinking water contaminated with chloride* and fluoride or ladened with insecticides*, pesticides, fungicides, and herbicides that are used to inflate profits in the production fruit and vegetables.

To ignore the practice of hygiene, results in the person robbing himself of living space and food. This means that someday, he will no longer have a home where he can live.

The Right to Beauty
People should like the world they are living in and enjoy taking care of it. Of course, beauty lies in the eye of the beholder. However, the exception is a demoted spirit, who favors those things that most people describe as ugly.

All people can contribute to the beauty of existence in their own way by means of personal care, pretty clothes and nice things that they surround themselves with, or on a larger scale, with good roads, esthetically pleasing buildings and nice parks.

No one wants to live in a grey and sad world for it is not a happy place.

The Right to Have Order
Order means that one can assign things to his environment and can recognize what these items are and for what they were intended. Furthermore, order encompasses things that are separated from one another and clearly identified.

No one likes to eat a cup of yoghurt and suddenly finds that he has screws in his mouth. Screws have no place in yoghurt!

Order also means that things have a set (specific) sequence and that the people who are affected by this sequence know about it. This is called a reglement, e.g. traffic control. Every activity in the work place or in a company has a sequence. It should be written down because it can be a valuable tool for the novice, who can refer to it or, given the possibility during the absence of an employee, maintain the usual workflow.

To have no order means to live in chaos. Chaos costs time, money and nerves!
Order only works when everyone knows and obeys it!

The Right to Competently Executed Work
Human existence is made possible through services and products. A state can only function by delivering good services and products. Products and services must do/

deliver/fulfill what they are supposed to do – a lawn mower is supposed to mow the lawn, and a worker who finishes an apprenticeship should be able to perform competently in that occupation.

At the end of the 19th century, products from Germany were so bad that they had to be marked "Made in Germany" as a warning to the consumer. The Germans learned from that and have since raised their working standards, and today, products from Germany are highly regarded and are preferred in comparison to products from other countries.

In fact, high quality work promotes the continued existence of the manufacturer, whereas faulty products are purchased only once! By lowering production and service standards, the employee puts himself and the company's reputation at risk.

When spending money to purchase something, it is only right to get what the money was spent on and not an inferior imitation, which is fraud. A scammer can be recognized by not keeping his promises.

One can contribute to a functioning environment by doing a good job and rejecting the bad!

The Right to Have Rights

Rights should ensure that life can exist in a physical universe. Life is life force + matter. Rights describe a framework for existence that ensures that through barriers and freedoms a living space of order is created, where the individual in comparison to others does not feel disfavored and where the symbionts* of humanity are protected.

Rights should be explained in such a way that they are unmistakably understood by anyone having learned how to read and write in the course of normal schooling. It should not require legal advice to interpret the laws so that they can be better understood. When a law is presented in writing, it should be backed up by case studies to clearly give a complete understanding.

The implementation of rights by law through the judicial system requires prudent reason. The impression should not arise that people are unduly constrained by the rights but that through the rights are assured a better existence where everyone in society considers themselves protected when abiding by the rules.

Rules should prevent damage to ensure a regulated procedure, which is only used when there is an imminent threat of danger or when the procedure itself requires regulation. Implementing rules without reason is oppression! People should be brought into a state of responsibility and understanding, so that they can reasonably implement rules.

Only if one knows his rights, can he claim them!

The Right to Safety

Human rights must be guaranteed as a country's constitutional rights. The citizen himself must know the rights, and these should be a part of a regular education.

In the case of a government violation, legal representation is to be provided, free of charge to the accused. If proof exists that the government violated the set right, an adjustment is initiated. In an extreme case, the government official is replaced when an adjustment proved to be unsuccessful. When a citizen violates an existing right, he is corrected. If the citizen proves to be completely intransigent and represents a danger to others either by bodily harm or by threat of life, or greatly endangers a peaceful existence, he must be removed from society.

The delinquent* must be given the opportunity to self-reflect in a restricted area, so that he can, on his own, change his mind and attitude without any physical or mental abuse. The moment he is found guilty, his rights are restricted, and he is granted only basic rights. The removal of the delinquent from society assures the safety of those who obey the laws and fulfill their obligations.

In a time of terror, the cry for more police becomes louder. But by what means and how will the police surveil the citizen? Are they supposed to keep an eye on everyone? An impossible task! The police cannot see into the mind of every individual to determine what he intends to do. **Generally, it is peaceful,** and there are only a few who terrorize people.

More police mean that the police also want to have something to do and will always find a sinner, be it the one who did not stop at the stop sign in accordance with the traffic law or the one who got a ticket for exceeding the speed limit by two mph while leaving town. Eventually there will be a hunt of decent citizens to justify an increased police presence due to fewer criminals.

Often it is so that when the police suddenly appear in a quiet and regulated neighborhood, one becomes insecure. To enforce order on everyone for the slightest rule violation displeases citizens and gives the police a bad reputation. When every citizen has a reasonable system of values in his head and then acts accordingly, it will bring about more safety than all the police in the world could provide!

The Right to a Fair Trial

Nothing causes more turmoil in a society than injustice. In the United States of America one can observe on a regular basis demonstrations by citizens protesting police actions when an African American gets shot by a police officer, and the officer is not charged with a crime.

However, to condemn someone based only on accusations is not representative of a nation of laws. During colonial times in the 17th century, in Salem, Massachusetts, USA, a little girl instigated numerous executions only because she accused people of witchcraft. During the witch trials, over 200 innocent people were accused of witchcraft, and 20 of them were executed ("Salem Witch Trials," n.d.). If someone makes accusations, then he must prove them, and the accusations must violate applicable law to be prosecuted. One is innocent until proven guilty!

Punishing someone simply for misconduct does not contribute to the improvement of the individual. In other words, we must know what the person did wrong and under what circumstances it happened. Was it intentional, out of carelessness or ignorance, or was the mistake made to avoid greater harm or damage? In any case, one will observe that if the individual commits an act intentionally, he has his reasons. So if one simply punishes the individual, he will feel violated by society and retaliate, which motivates and justifies his next act.

In an unjust and biased environment, there are unjust actions. By establishing a just and educated environment that observes human rights, one has a foundation to rehabilitate the individual, so that he can change his attitude and can contribute to a just environment by applying himself.

If something really went wrong, the liable party should have a right to make restitution without being punished, and if the matter was taken care of, then his transgression should be forgiven. Of what use is revenge and retaliation? These only bring forth further revenge and retribution, and only so that human beings have some sort of satisfaction. It should be understood that every transgression carries consequences, some immediate and some long-term. In the final analysis, everyone has the potential of being negatively affected by the transgressor's actions.

The Right to Have Property

Every human being should have the opportunity to acquire as much property as he himself can maintain! Exceptions are company or government property and public institutions, which are used by various people and thus require a bit more organization.

It is not acceptable that the one who has unlimited financial resources also has unrestricted access to real property– it simply is again the rule by right of the strongest. One could employ countless lawyers just to keep the courts busy and at some point, force the opposing party to give up because they can no longer pay the accumulating legal costs.

The human being himself wants to have something, and the things that he has should belong to him. When things belong to no one, one will find that no one will take care of them, and they fall into a state of disrepair. Therefore, property carries the responsibility to keep it in order – property requires responsibility! But it is also the case that the human being is held liable for his property, thus ensuring that things are properly maintained, and this not only applies to the direct possessions, but also to planet Earth!

Ownership is a right. To just take away something from someone, or to somehow arrange it to be taken away, or to get rid of something due to wrong information, is theft. Only if the owner offers goods* out of his own free will and without coercion or manipulation, or if he wants to give them away without exchange, can another have the goods.

The Right to Freedom, Privacy and Individuality

Freedom means to have no or few barriers. By living in a lawful state, the human being is given a playing field with rules of conduct, whereby the court is the referee and decides right* and wrong, or whether there is a rule violation or not.

However, humans should also be given the opportunity to operate outside of the rules mandated by the state when there are demarcated areas where other rules apply, such as an official boxing match, where bodily harm is accepted; or, an official motor sport competition, in which the overtaking and speed regulations are designed differently.

Likewise, humans have a private sphere in which they can do many things, but without being a public nuisance, e.g. music being too loud, thereby disturbing the neighbor. The private sphere is a legally protected area, and the state authorities can only intervene when the public order is disturbed, or when danger threatens. Intervention is by a court order or by a search warrant - except when danger is imminent.

The human being should have a right to live his own life without restriction- at least outside working hours where he is not committed to the job-related interests of the employer. Thus, the human being should have a temporal freedom in which he is able to recuperate or to devote himself to his interests. By living one's life, one should be somewhat careful not to overstrain the reality* of his fellow human beings.

Extreme idiosyncrasies* lead to exclusion. Individualism is when one does not feel obligated to accept certain mannerism due to group pressure, religious or ideological reasons. Some say that if they copied something somewhere and then imitated it, that that it is a form of individualism – be that as it may. As long as one does things of his own free will, without being coerced or manipulated, it should be alright.

The human being should have the opportunity to open a new demarcated area with his own rules, whereby the community developed therein must be aware of the new rules and agree with them. It should be made clear to everyone that if the human rights that are promulgated are not observed, trouble will arise!

Mind you, the pursuit of one's own independent state with its own rules and laws can easily backfire. No state easily allows the separation of any of its land and any of its population, even by demand of the population. The ringleaders are quickly put behind bars, as was the case with Puigdemont*.

Freedom can only be attained when one is strong enough and has sufficient military power to fight for and to defend it!

The Right to Defense
A person must have the ability to defend himself when he or his rights are violated. Of course, he can only defend his rights when he knows them! An oppressive environment cannot make the person aware of his rights. It leads to slogans* like: "Ignorance does not protect against punishment!"

The Right to Receive Aid
People should help each other. It should be a balanced giving and taking, and if one is unable to adequately help someone in the foreseeable future, then the helper must compensate the one in need monetarily, unless the helper legally relieved himself of the obligation, or there was an unforeseen emergency. It is not acceptable that the one with the thickest wallet can buy most of the aid.

Furthermore, the state benefits through taxes collected on the provided services and products. Things become expensive and sometimes so expensive that if one "helps" someone with a product or a service, the one being helped feels hoodwinked!

An unrestrained accumulation of capital resources in the private sector creates a second-class society with people who have lots of money and people who have little. Money itself is a means of payment provided by the state, and the state itself should contribute to a fair distribution. The past has demonstrated that when social differences result in income inequality, dissatisfaction and the resistance of underprivileged citizens results. This can be prevented!

The Right to Religion
I am not talking about a cult* or a belief system existing of tenets* that serves to calm a fictitious* deity, cautions against acts that incur his wrath and promises life after death in some fictional heaven to lead a heavenly existence - that is superstition!

How much freedom of action does one have when he submits to an unobjectionable belief system that represents medieval values? It pins the person down in that time, not allowing progress! Rules should lead to the best possible survival, and for this, the rules themselves must be flexible because the human being changes and because the human being changes the environment in which he wants to live. Rights will change when the human being and the environment change!

Everyone should be free to decide whether he wants to submit himself to such a belief system or not. At least there should be a neutral "religious education" in public schools, in which the creeds and goals of various religions are discussed, and not where a certain religion is forced upon students, as it is currently the case in Germany - one should be able to choose a religion freely after one learns about them.

Religion should serve the human being to recognize his spirituality and his brotherhood with this universe. It should show him that he can exist separately from matter and provide him knowledge and techniques to achieve this. It should show him what this brotherhood signifies and how he interacts with all parts of the world and this universe.

A religion is then justifiable as a religion when it is in accordance with the laws of the state, and the state law is in accordance with human rights, and all these are in accordance with the natural law. When these things conflict, problems will arise - and we see a world as it is now!

The person himself, which is the life force, should have the right to invigorate matter or not. There are circumstances by which the body is so strongly affected, e.g. illness, mutilation, genetic disorder, etc., that the person's existence in this body appears not worth living any longer. If the person makes that decision, then he should be granted the right to separate from this body.

The Obligation

There is an obligation resulting from the above rights to see that these rights gain validity and get implemented on behalf of each individual. People always speak freely about their rights to which they are entitled when living together with others. However, this coexistence not only brings along rights but also obligations; therefore, committing to any relationship is a giving and taking.

Instead of focusing on one's rights, one should, above all, think about what one can do for this society, so that this society can function. Mind you, this society only functions when one contributes something to the society. In this regard, the word *right* could be replaced with the word *obligation* at the beginning of every paragraph. If everyone felt obliged to implement the above rights and would actively do it, then what would oppose a happy existence?

Thus, a plea to the reader: Be a role model and set an example by putting this document into practice. By encouraging others, the "Human Rights and Obligations," will soon become a reality.

Closing Remarks

One can recognize something bad when one knows what is good. When one knows the good and desires it, one can pursue it.

A common togetherness requires common thoughts. It requires a single foundation upon which every individual in a society can agree and that meets with his approval and for which he vouches.

Equal rights and equal obligation for all, no exceptions!

Glossary

asterisk: a star like symbol (*) used in printing to indicate footnotes, omissions, etc.

barbaric environment: In 1791, the American Congress passed the "Bill of Rights," the 10 additional articles (amendments) to the United States Constitution, which guaranteed the citizen inalienable fundamental rights. The "Bill of Rights" was born in the spirit of an embattled country allowing the citizens to bear arms ("Second Amendment," n.d.). Today, in the 21st century, the former fights are fought, but the citizen still has the right to bear arms. It is questionable whether one feels safer being armed, since other citizens also have weapons. Thus, the power of the police is severely limited, since they must consider dangerous resistance, in the case of an altercation. The police officer by responding to dangerous areas has to fear for his life every day. What was once thought to be for the protection of the citizen has turned to his detriment today! In 2017, more than 15,000 people were killed in more than 60,000 registered shootings in the United States ("Number of recorded incidents," n.d.).

chloride, fluoride: chemical substances that are added in low concentration to the drinking water in various countries. Chlorine is used for disinfection and fluoride for the prevention of tooth decay - both have side effects.

code: any set of principles or rules of conduct.

construct of thought: memorized information by the individual and the conclusions thereof, available for further computations/thought processes.

cult: (a) a group of people with a religious, philosophical or cultural identity sometimes viewed as a sect, often existing on the margins of society and being exploitative towards its members. (b) devoted attachment to, or extravagant admiration for, a person, principle, or lifestyle.

decree: an official order, edict, or decision, as of a church, government, court, etc.

delinquent: person who is failing or neglecting to do what duty or law requires.

depressed: feeling or characterized by sadness or dejection.

Eldorado: an area that offers excellent opportunities for development.

extrinsic: being, coming, or acting from the outside.

factor: a contributor to something.

fact: something that actually took place, or that is really true.

fears of existence: being afraid not to master one's own life –the environment being too challenging, or too threatening.

fictitious: existing only in the imagination; fanciful; unreal.

food: In the United States and Europe, laws are passed to reduce the production of food. Farmers create scarcity by destroying food to keep prices stable! It is not some shortage as far as resources and production are concerned, but a misguided policy, based on a lack of management, which is manifested in its inability to distribute the produced goods fairly inside the country. This artificially controls prices, making the poor poorer and the rich richer!

fortune, small: Cancer treatment can cost $10,000 annually, even up to $750,000 with a statistical life prolongation of about one month. One day in the hospital can cost $2,000 (2014), and surgery for a broken leg, between $17,000 and $35,000. Medical care is a multi-billion-dollar business! (Ellison 2016; Kantarjian, H., Steensma, D., Sanjuan, J.D., Elshaug, A., & Light, D., 2014; "Nusinersen," n.d.; "The 6 most expensive," n.d.)

goods: things that can be purchased and sold; merchandise.

ideologies: the doctrines, opinions, or way of thinking of an individual, class, etc.; specifically, the body of ideas on which a particular political, economic, or social system is based.

idiosyncrasy: any personal peculiarity, mannerism, etc.

impoverishment of people: Poverty is widespread among minors. In Germany, 3.7 million children and adolescents are dependent on youth welfare ("Poverty in Germany," 2017). The equal number of pensioners live in Germany with a statutory pension of less than 300 euros per month. Six million pensioners receive up to 500 euros. Thirteen million senior citizens, around 72%, received a pension of up to € 1,000 a month in 2012 ("Statutory Pension," n.d.). In Germany, the legal definition of poor describes a single person who earns less than 917 euros net a month (Finkenwirth & Diemand, 2017).

In the United States, the official poverty rate for 2017 is 13.9%, an estimated 39.7 million Americans, according to the official measure (Fontenot, Semega, & Kollar, 2018). The poverty threshold in 2017 for a single person in the US was $12,060; $16,240 for two persons in the household; $20,420 for three persons; and $24,600 for four persons (Wissman, 2017)

Indo-Germanic: circa 4,000 BC ancient language from which most languages descended.

insecticides, pesticides, fungicides, and herbicides: A substance or agent used to kill insects, germs, fungi or weeds. These remedies kill life and, with strong concentration, also humans!

inversion: a reversal of something, e.g. from good to bad.

manipulate: to consciously influence or manage shrewdly or deviously.

money: something generally accepted as a medium of exchange, a measure of value, or a means of payment legitimized by a government. The government brings money into circulation and determines by laws who has how much (the amount), e.g. income tax, minimum wage, rent control, etc. The money is regulated to keep its value stable. The poor remain poor, and the worker is kept "hungry" so that he always has to work because the majority of the people in the state have little money. Therefore, they cannot spend a lot, which keeps prices low.

oracle: a person, such as a priestess, through whom a deity is believed to speak, a prophecy.

pestilence: also called the Black Death; actually, a rodent disease transmitted from rat fleas to humans and from humans to humans via the bacillus Yersinia pestis. The disease is still around in some parts of the world. It resulted in the deaths of an estimated 75 to 200 million people in Eurasia, peaking in Europe from 1347 to 1351 ("Black Death," n.d.; "Yersenia Pestis," n.d.).

Puigdemont, Carles: former president of Catalonia, Spain, who fought for Catalonia's independence ("Escalation in Catalonia," n.d.).

rationalization: The economical design of work processes that utilizes automation to improve productivity and quality, decreasing the need for human labor. Where in the past 100 workers were needed on an assembly line, now the same work can be done by a robot and two specialists. Similarly, a computer replaces numerous administrative employees. The human being rationalizes himself away, where the machines are meant to facilitate the work of the human being. If the human being is to finance his life with money, then he must also have the opportunity to earn money!

reality: degree of a general agreement, which determines what is "normal."

revised: read over carefully and corrected, improved, or updated where necessary.

right and wrong: this is a matter of reason, meaning the doing of or the refraining from actions that have more benefits than disadvantages for one and one's symbionts now and in the future.

slogan: a word or phrase embodying a principle or precept.

symbiont: an organism living in a state of symbiosis. Symbiosis is co-existing for a mutual use.

tarot cards: a deck of cards used by fortune tellers and card readers to help predict the future.

tenet: a belief or principle that is held by a group as being true.

zeitgeist: the spirit of the age; trend of thought and feeling in a period.

References

Black Death. (n.d.). In *Wikipedia*. Retrieved from https://en.wikipedia.org/wiki/Black_Death.

Ellison, A. (2016, January 13). Average cost per inpatient day across 50 states. *Becker's Healthcare*. Retrieved from https://www.beckershospitalreview.com/finance/average-cost-per-inpatient-day-across-50-states-2016.html

Escalation in Catalonia: Judge issues arrest warrant against Puigdemont. (n.d.). *Online Focus*. Retrieved from https://www.focus.de/politik/ausland/katalonien-konflikt-im-news-ticker-puigdemont-erscheint-nicht-in-spanien-vor-gericht_id_7791691.html.

Finkenwirth, A., & Diemand, S. (2017, March 2). How poor are the Germans? *Zeit Online*. Retrieved from https://www.zeit.de/wirtschaft/2017-03/armutsbericht-2017-deutschland-paritaetischer-wohlfahrtsverband-faq.

Fontenot, K., Semega, J., & Kollar, M. (2018, September 12). *Income and poverty in the United States: 2017* (Report Number P60-263). Retrieved from https://www.census.gov/library/publications/2018/demo/p60-263.html .

Great Pacific garbage patch. (n.d.). In *Wikipedia*. Retrieved from https://en.wikipedia.org/wiki/Great _Pacific_garbage_patch.

Kantarjian, H., Steensma, D., Sanjuan, J.D., Elshaug, A., & Light, D. (2014, May 6). High cancer drug prices in the United States: Reasons and proposed solutions. *Journal of Oncology Practice*. Retrieved from http://ascopubs.org/doi/full/10.1200/jop.2013.001351.

Number of recorded incidents, deaths and injuries from firearms in the US from 2014 to 2018 (until 5 September). (n.d.). *Statista*. Retrieved from https://de.statista.com/statistik/daten/studie/579175/umfrage/vorfaelle-und-todesfaelle-durch-schusswaffen-in-den-usa/

Nusinserin (n.d.) In *Wikipedia*. Retrieved from https://en.wikipedia.org/wiki/Nusi nersen.

Poverty in Germany. (2017, March 20). *Spiegel Online*. Retrieved from http://www. spiegel.de/panorama/gesellschaft/kinderamut-mehr-als-jeder-vierte-min derjaehrige-laut-jungendhilfe-ausegrentz-a-1139624.html.

Salem witch trials. (n.d.). In *Wikipedia*. Retrieved from https://en.wikipedia.org/ wiki/Salem_witch_ trials.

Second Amendment to the United States Constitution. (n.d.). In *Wikipedia*. Ret rieved from https://en.wikipedia.org/wiki/Second_Amendment_to_the_Uni ted_States_Constitution.

The 6 most expensive anticancer drugs. (2017, February 27). *Ideal Magazin*. Retrie ved from https://www.ideal-versicherung.de/magazin/die-6-teuersten-krebsmedikamente/

Statutory pension in Germany. (n.d.). In *Wikipedia*. Retrieved from https:// de.wikipedia.org/wiki/ Gesetzliche_Rentenversicherung_(Deutschland).

Wissman, L. (2017, February 7). 2017 poverty level guidelines. *PeopleKeep*. Ret rieved from https://www.peoplekeep.com/blog/2017-federal-poverty-le vel-guidelines.

Yersinia pestis. (n.d.). In *Wikipedia*. Retrieved from https://en.wikipedia.org/wiki/ Yersinia_pestis.

About the Author

I, Wolfgang Fries, was born in St. Wendel/ Saarland, Germany, on January 16, 1966. I had a standard education that included technical school. Afterward, I served five years in the Bundeswehr (German army) until 1994, when I started working as a stucco master, an occupation that enriched my life. I was easily able to form social contacts and was still well-liked after work. By forming a few friendships, I felt a social bond with others.

Unfortunately, I had to stop this nice work. As it turned out, bad things can lead to a good result. If I were not sitting in a wheelchair, I never would have written all of this. During a disastrous accident with the motorcycle, I broke my spine and since then have been permanently paralyzed.

But there is something in life everyone should know: Life itself. During all the work one does, and all the good times one enjoys, one should never forget this.

So I went and wrote everything down. I see it as my responsibility to my fellow human beings, because nobody came to me explaining things in a way that I could understand them.

I hope for the reader that through the knowledge in this book, he has better standards for life, to make better decisions in life, to live a better life, for himself and his symbionts!

Philosophie des Lebens - Das Buch der Grundlagen -

Was sind die Grundlagen des Daseins? Welche Geisteshaltung bedarf es in der heutigen Zeit um im Leben bestehen zu können, um Glück und Wohlergehen zu erfahren? Was ist wichtig zu wissen?

Der Mensch selbst, als denkendes Wesen ist der Ansicht, dass seine mächtigste Waffe der Verstand ist. Aufgrund seiner Fähigkeit zu denken hat er sich die Erde zum Untertan gemacht. Und tatsächlich, das Denken bestimmt das Handeln des Menschen, der Mensch ist nur so stabil wie sein Gedanke.

Der Gedanke selbst fußt auf Grundlagen die bestimmend dazu sind, wie man überlebt. So versucht der Mensch sich selbst, sein Denken und Handeln, die Welt um sich herum zu verstehen.

Verstehen: Was ist wichtiger als Verstehen selbst?

Grundlagen komprimiert verpackt, in kurzen Texten dargestellt. Mehr als 200 Essays führen den Leser zu mehr Verstehen im Leben und über das Leben selbst, sei es nun über den Menschen, das Denken, Glücklichsein, Beziehung, Lernen, Beruf, den Ursprung von Krankheiten, gesellschaftliches Dasein, Religion, Politik oder Freiheit.

Die Probleme des Menschen werden von der Ursache her geschildert und Lösungen angeboten. Es macht einen Unterschied dieses Wissen zu haben und sich dadurch selbst zu helfen.

„Philosophie des Lebens – Das Buch der Grundlagen" ist der Gesamt-Band welcher die Bücher „Meine Philosophie"; „Lernen wie man lernt, lernen wie man versteht"; „Eine glückliche Beziehung führen"; „Verstehen: Der Band aus einzelnen Werken"; „Rückführung – Einführung und Kurzanleitung" in einem Buch vereint.

Als Taschenbuch oder als Bibliotheken-Ausgabe im extra stabilen Hardcover-Format und Fadenbindung herausgegeben.

Philosophie des Lebens - Das Buch der Grundlagen -; 656 Seiten, 2017.

ISBN: **978-3-7357-8561-9** - Hardcover
ISBN: **978-3-7460-2923-8** - Taschenbuch